DAD'S
PLAYBOOK

DAD'S PLAYBOOK

WISDOM FOR FATHERS

— *FROM THE* —

GREATEST COACHES OF ALL TIME

BY TOM LIMBERT

FOREWORD BY HALL OF FAME QUARTERBACK
STEVE YOUNG

CHRONICLE BOOKS
SAN FRANCISCO

To my wife, Eve, who shows me every day
the value of enjoying your child.
And to our son, Leo, who makes it easy.

Library of Congress Cataloging-in-Publication Data:
Limbert, Tom.
    Dad's playbook : wisdom for fathers from the greatest coaches of all time /
Tom Limbert.
        p. cm.
    ISBN 978-1-4521-0251-1
    1. Fatherhood. 2. Father and child. 3. Parenting. 4. Coaches (Athletics)—
Quotations. I. Title.

HQ756.L53 2012
306.874'2—dc23

2011018894

Manufactured in China

MIX
Paper from
responsible sources
FSC™ C104723

Design by Angelo R. Alcasabas

20 19 18 17 16 15

Chronicle Books LLC
680 Second Street
San Francisco, CA 94107
www.chroniclebooks.com

-CONTENTS-

FOREWORD

By Steve Young

My father made me the man I am today. So it was only fitting that he introduced me when I was inducted into the Pro Football Hall of Fame. I would never have made it there without his support and guidance. My dad, like any coach, has always stressed the fundamentals. He taught me responsibility, accountability, and the importance of hard work. As a teenager, when I wanted to start borrowing the car, my dad agreed under the condition I get a job so I could afford to put gas in it. Juggling a full load at school and the demands of three sports, I somehow found enough time to work at a local ice-cream store. It is lessons like these that have stuck with me. Though my father was tough, he was always in my corner, teaching me the value of hard work. He taught me that the most valuable lessons in life are learned through adversity. His motto on adversity was to always go through it, not around it. You don't learn by sitting back and watching. It is this strong foundation that gave me the ability to persist and achieve success in all facets of my life. When I became the starting quarterback for the 49ers and confronted adversity and doubt, I feared calling my dad. I knew he wouldn't give me an easy way out. I knew he'd say, "Endure to the end, Steve." Like any great coach, he is always trying to prepare me for challenges and encouraging me to reach my potential.

At home I was blessed with a strong role model for a father, and on the field I was equally blessed to have the best coaches an athlete could ask for. Each and every lesson a coach taught me has shaped me into the person and father I am today. At BYU, LaVell Edwards taught me the value of teamwork and execution: If you find the right people in the right places working together for common goals, success is inevitable. This power of unity certainly applies in a family.

In San Francisco, Bill Walsh added to what my father taught me about accountability. When I replaced Joe Montana and things weren't going well, I started to believe the people who were saying it was all my fault. As the oldest sibling in a large family, I was used to taking responsibility for others. But Bill came to me and said, "Look, you're stealing accountability from others. And teams will play much better if everyone is held accountable. So figure out ways where you can take your piece, and make sure others are allowed to take their piece as well." Although he was honest and direct, he said it in a way that was empathetic and nonjudgmental. He helped me understand that, in a team setting, everyone has to hold themselves accountable. It was clear he wanted what was best for me and for our team.

Now that I am a father of four, I find myself passing along to my children the values and messages learned from my father and coaches. My wife, Barb, and I both teach accountability and encourage unity. We instill our values in our children through patient and honest dialogue. When our older children want to play video games, they have to earn their time. There are certain things they can do to earn their time, and homework is not one of them. We tell them plainly that education is its own benefit. They earn their time by doing chores or performing actions that benefit the family. When our boys argue, we encourage them to talk to each other and work things out together. We tell them they have a long future together and will be best friends for life. Like my parents and coaches did for me, my wife and I make an effort to help our children understand their experiences and learn from them. It's what leaders do.

This book is all about leadership. Tom has collected more than one hundred quotes from some of the greatest coaches of all time and applied their principles and lessons to fatherhood. Each and every quote teaches and inspires. When Coach Krzyzewski advises us, "Don't worry about losing, think about winning," the lesson in self-confidence and attitude is obvious. It certainly applies to our role as fathers, where confidence is key, and it's also a great way to teach our children to think. You have to see the glass as half full. You have to keep moving forward. Adversity is inevitable. Faith is essential.

Tom applies these lessons and many more to our role as fathers. In this book, Tom inspires us to create an honest and supportive environment for our children. He encourages us to explain limits and rules to children and to lead by example. He reminds us that much like coaches, we are teachers. It's not lost on me. The first thing I did when I got to the microphone on the day of my induction into the Pro Football Hall of Fame was thank my parents. "Since becoming a father several years ago," I explained, "I have become more fully appreciative of the role of mothers and fathers in life, and I thank both my parents for being such great examples and teachers to me." Now when our children encounter challenges, my wife and I do our best to get down to their level and explain why challenges are important, what matters, and why.

If there were a Hall of Fame for husbands and dads, I'd make it my number one goal to get there. On the day I was inducted into the Pro Football Hall of Fame, just before I concluded my speech by thanking my wife, Barb, for all the sacrifices she has made for our family, I made a statement that I hope I can live up to. I said, "I sincerely love my family and know that being a Hall of Fame husband and dad is what will eventually define my life." It's a lofty goal I know, but I believe a worthy one to shoot for. As Tom reminds us in this book, if we set lofty goals, our children will follow. *Dad's Playbook* can help you be a Hall of Fame father for your children.

NO WHISTLE REQUIRED

ow many times have you heard a player refer to his coach as a "father figure"? The parallels between fathering and coaching are undeniable. Just as a coach wants his players and team to excel, you want your child and family to excel. Coaches—like parents—are charged with the important task of teaching, guiding, and motivating. And both must also walk the fine line between providing love and support and instilling discipline.

As teachers, leaders, and motivators, we as fathers can learn a lot from both the mistakes and triumphs of coaches. In this book I have collected more than one hundred of the most relevant and inspirational quotes from some of the greatest coaches of all time. These men have enjoyed tremendous admiration and success, and from them we can learn a great deal about leadership, confidence, discipline, unity, and motivation. Although none of the coaches intended these quotes to be applied to the task of parenting, when you read them in that context, the lessons and messages are unmistakably congruent and impactful.

Both coaching and parenting are extremely challenging jobs. It is only natural for us to admire a coach who exhibits strong leadership qualities. Occasionally we bear witness to a coach's weaker moments and are reminded that these esteemed leaders are, in fact, human. For instance, just a few days before I planned to submit my first draft of this book to my editor, I took a breather to catch some Monday night football. It was October 2010, and the Eagles were visiting the winless 49ers. There I was trying to get my mind off my deadline, when Mike Singletary got all up in the grill of his still-developing quarterback, Alex Smith, following a stalled drive. Sitting in the comfort of our couches at home, sheltered from the cascade of boos, myself and millions of other football fans witnessed a discouraged leader lose his composure in the heat of the moment. Singletary could not hide his disappointment and frustration. He didn't really seem to want to. When other players and coaches intervened to quell the escalating tension, I couldn't help but wonder if Singletary had ever read any Paul "Bear" Bryant quotes—"Find your own self in anything that goes bad" came to mind. If he had, wouldn't he have assumed the responsibility for the errant passes and offered encouragement and insight instead? It was painfully obvious that the pressure of his job was taking a toll on him, deterring his ability to communicate and lead effectively. I know coaching at the NFL level is no easy job, but I found it ironic that the very week I planned to submit material to my editor about how dads should try be more like coaches, a coach's weaker moment was nationally televised.

Let's be clear: I'm not casting stones or pointing fingers at Mike Singletary (he's much, much bigger than me). My wife would be happy to testify that if a camera followed me around, viewers would be afforded plenty of scenarios in which I lose my cool too. Furthermore, as a Cowboys fan, I would love it if Wade Phillips furrowed his brow or clapped his hands just one time. Expressions like these have their place in the realm of sports and coaching at times, but not so much in parenting. Somewhere in between Wade Phillips and Mike Singletary lies the balance of effective leadership—a balance that applies to both sports and parenting. Of course, the relationship between a child and a father is not exactly like that of a coach and player. My point is simply that similar lessons and principles apply.

Two days after the Alex Smith/Mike Singletary confrontation, as I was getting ready to submit my final draft, I read an interview with former Oakland Raiders' coach John Madden. He was asked about the Monday night confrontation between Singletary and Smith. "A lot of things go on in a game you're not proud of as a coach," Madden explained. "That's really not part of coaching—sometimes I worry about that. I see youth football and high school football and coaches yelling at players—and I cringe when I see it. I think people get the picture that that's what coaching is and, believe me, that's not what coaching is." As I read on, I was delighted to hear a Hall of

Famer articulate what coaching is all about: "You have to coach, you have to teach, you have to strategize, you have to encourage. That's what coaching is, not the opposite." Boom.

And there you have it, the spirit of *Dad's Playbook* in a nutshell. As fathers, we too have to teach, plan, and encourage. We have to coach 'em up. This book doesn't promote yelling at your children or motivating them with fear. Rather, it champions being a leader and inspiring your child to do his best, creating a supportive team environment in which he feels respected and loved. Grouped into five chapters—Lead and Inspire, Believe and Praise, Love and Respect, Teach and Learn, and Live and Enjoy—the quotations in this book can guide the way to being a positive presence and a true mentor for your children. These enduring lessons from sports' most celebrated leaders will help you create a supportive, winning dynamic in your home.

By the time fall turned to winter, both Wade Phillips and Mike Singletary had been fired from their head coaching positions. The Cowboys promoted Jason Garrett, who brought enthusiasm, clear boundaries, and accountability to the team—three key ingredients that were missing under Wade Phillips. The players responded to the new leadership with their own renewed energy and cohesiveness. Singletary was fired after a game in which he had another sideline blowup with another of his quarterbacks. When asked about the heated confrontation, Singletary confessed, "I don't really know about coaching etiquette. I am sure that there is a right way and a wrong way in today's rules of being politically correct." A masterful leader on the field in his playing days and a renowned motivational speaker, Singletary failed to realize that leading and motivating people is every bit as much about respect and communication as it is about bringing energy and enthusiasm. These facts are timeless and universal, and go much deeper than political correctness.

You're a role model, and you might as well use it to your advantage. If you bring energy and enthusiasm to each day—and to each relationship—your children will witness this and emulate it. Jack Harbaugh was a football coach for forty-two years. He used to drop his sons off at elementary school and say, "Now go out there and attack this day with an enthusiasm unknown to mankind." Both his sons, Jim and John, are now head coaches in the NFL. You might think that's mere coincidence, but I think there's more to it than that. Whether your child is forty years old or forty days old, you can influence her either negatively or positively. You know it. Accept it. Embrace it. Speak from your heart—you have a direct line to hers. You don't need a whistle.

LEAD

- AND -

INSPIRE

You've heard the phrase "leadership starts at the top"—but have you thought about it in terms of your own family? Well guess who's on top? Whether you're conscious of it or not, you lead and inspire with both your words and your actions. You decide what kind of values to instill, which goals to set, and how to go about reaching those goals. You have a tremendous impact on your family. Through your example, every day you show your children how to treat each other, how to handle adversity, and how to get things done. Make no mistake about it, it is a huge responsibility. But as the best coaches have shown us, the price of greatness is responsibility.

When you demonstrate the value of hard work and the importance of always doing your best, you give your children something to aspire to. What are your goals for your family? Do you expect everyone to take care of each other and support one another? Like a coach, articulate those expectations in no uncertain terms. If you don't declare it then who will? Remember that no goal was ever reached without being set in the first place. Tony Dorsett echoes: "To succeed you need to find something to hold on to, something to motivate you, something to inspire you." Help your child find that something. Perhaps even be that something for your child. Do you wish for your child to always do her best? Then you must walk the talk and, while you're at it, talk the walk. If you want your child to be caring and thoughtful, then be caring and thoughtful. If you truly want your child to be polite, then be polite to her and to others. Your child will learn to be patient and express gratitude if you show her how. Get your kids to buy in to the team concept by exemplifying team ideals and values like support and encouragement. Just as a coach outlines plays and defines goals, it's up to you to create a game plan and provide explanations.

When your child encounters challenges, be there to listen and help him find solutions. Resist the urge to fix everything yourself. Meet your child where he is and gently lead him to where he wants to be. Strongly inspire him to go where he needs to go. That is the essence of coaching, teaching, and parenting. Success will be inevitable. The proverbial ball is in your court. Embrace the responsibility of being your child's greatest role model by being your child's greatest role model. You will be a genuine leader and a true inspiration.

Find your own picture, your own self, in anything that goes bad. It's awfully easy to mouth off at your staff or chew out players, but if it's bad, and you're the head coach, you're responsible. If we have an intercepted pass, I threw it. If we get a punt blocked, I caused it. It's up to the head coach to assume his responsibility.

BEAR BRYANT

Leaders aren't born, they are made. And they are made just like anything else—through hard work. And that's the price we'll have to pay to achieve that goal, or any goal.

VINCE LOMBARDI

I had the greatest luxury in life—the love of a mother and father. I can never say I was emotionally or psychologically deprived by a man who had to work his ass off and make certain we had security. That's the reason I'm proud to be called John Thompson. It doesn't have anything to do with me winning a damn thing at Georgetown. It has more to do with what that man did.

JOHN THOMPSON

Don't coach mad.

RICK PITINO

If you whoop and holler all the time, the players get used to it.

BEAR BRYANT

— — —

Managing is like holding a dove in your hand. Squeeze too hard and you kill it, not hard enough and it flies away.

TOMMY LASORDA

Great effort springs naturally from great attitude.

PAT RILEY

— — —

What makes a good coach?
Complete dedication.

GEORGE HALAS

— — —

The man who complains about the way the ball bounces is likely the one who dropped it.

LOU HOLTZ

Leadership is a matter of having people look at you and gain confidence, seeing how you react. If you're in control, they're in control.

TOM LANDRY

Young people need models, not critics.

JOHN WOODEN

You can't win them all.

CONNIE MACK

— — —

A good coach will make players see what they can be rather than what they are.

ARA PARSEGHIAN

One man practicing sportsmanship is far better than fifty preaching it.

KNUTE ROCKNE

— — —

Show class, have pride, and display character. If you do, winning takes care of itself.

BEAR BRYANT

— — —

Leadership is difficult. It is a lonely responsibility. The best leaders are servants. It is always about others.

DALE BROWN

Treat a person as he is, and he will remain as he is. Treat a person as if he were where he could be and should be, and he will become what he could be and should be.

JIMMY JOHNSON

Never quit. It is the easiest cop-out in the world. Set a goal and don't quit until you attain it. When you do attain it, set another goal, and don't quit until you reach it. Never quit.

BEAR BRYANT

Ability is what you're capable of doing.
Motivation determines what you do.
Attitude determines how well you do it.

LOU HOLTZ

— — —

I wish all there was to it was to take a chair and throw it into a blackboard or something, and then all of a sudden everything is [fine]. I don't think that's really the answer.

BILL BELICHICK

My responsibility is leadership, and the minute I get negative, that is going to have an influence on my team.

DON SHULA

BELIEVE

- AND -

PRAISE

Praise has long been a controversial subject among parenting experts. Some recommend lavishing praise on children. Others warn against offering too much. And yet, while the debate carries on, what's hardly ever touched upon is what's needed before praise to achieve success in children: motivation. And the best way to motivate your children is to believe in them. When you believe in your child, she will in turn believe in herself—and ultimately succeed. Research can't quantify this. It can't be measured or tested in a lab, but we know it's true. Coaches demonstrate this principle all the time, and it's even more relevant and crucial in parenting. Start believing in your child the day she is born, and continue believing in her as long as you live. Your belief will strengthen her determination and drive.

Have great expectations for your child—but make sure they are realistic. When you share these expectations in a warm and supportive manner, your child will lend a willing ear. He will also be more willing to follow your lead if you have equally high expectations for yourself and always strive to do your best. Make it a goal to make each other proud. By planting a seed of confidence in your child, you will inspire him to reach his true potential. Show and tell him that you believe in him—that you are in his corner. Ultimately great expectations will blossom into celebrated accomplishments.

Of course, we all know that challenges, failures, and disappointment are very much a part of childhood and life itself. There will be times when your child is cautious, fearful, and anxious. This is when your belief comes in, when you tell your child that you have faith in her abilities. Try these four words on for size: "You can do it." How about four more: "I know you can."

So now what of praise? Should we listen to those experts who warn against overpraising? Should we, as parents, act as emotionless robots when we witness our child's first steps? Will we stunt our child's development if we dare say "good job" when he brings home an A? My sources say no. But it is important to be thoughtful and even judicious with our praise. Research has shown that the most effective praise is specific. This holds true in business, sports, inter-personal relationships, and parenting. But I might add that it is just as important to be genuine and natural. In short, be real. Might as well, since he'll know if you're not anyway. When your child strives to do his best and makes you proud, acknowledge and commend his effort. Open the lines of honest communication and tell him how he made you feel. Talk about why doing your best is so satisfying and beneficial.

When you strive to do your best, you give your child something to aspire to and believe in. Empower your child with your belief and encouragement. She will learn to believe in herself and be motivated to pursue her dreams with confidence. You will discover more and more opportunities to shower her with your genuine congratulations.

My father gave me the greatest gift anyone could give another person: He believed in me.

JIM VALVANO

Success is peace of mind, which is a direct result of self-satisfaction in knowing you did your best to become the best you are capable of becoming.

JOHN WOODEN

— — —

I don't think anything is unrealistic if you believe you can do it. I think if you are determined enough and willing to pay the price, you can get it done.

MIKE DITKA

Nothing is more effective than sincere, accurate praise, and nothing is more lame than a cookie-cutter compliment.

BILL WALSH

The difference between a successful person and others is not a lack of strength, not a lack of knowledge, but rather a lack of will.

VINCE LOMBARDI

Be slow to criticize and quick to commend.

JOHN WOODEN

Goals should be realistic, attainable, and shared among all members of the team.

MIKE KRZYZEWSKI

— — —

There are only two options regarding commitment. You're either *in* or you're *out*. There is no such thing as life in-between.

PAT RILEY

— — —

I do believe in praising that which deserves to be praised.

DEAN SMITH

Nobody who ever gave his best regretted it.

GEORGE HALAS

The difference between the impossible and the possible lies in a man's determination.

TOMMY LASORDA

As teachers and coaches, we must remember that when mere winning is our only goal, we are doomed to disappointment and failure. But when our goal is to try to win, when our focus is on preparation and sacrifice and effort instead of on numbers on a scoreboard, then we will never lose.

MIKE KRZYZEWSKI

The first step toward creating an improved future is developing the ability to envision it. Vision will ignite the fire of passion that fuels our commitment to do *whatever it takes* to achieve excellence. Only *vision* allows us to transform dreams of greatness into reality of achievement through human action. *Vision* has no boundaries and knows no limits. Our *vision* is what we become in life.

TONY DUNGY

We should be dreaming. We grew up as kids having dreams, but now we're too sophisticated as adults, as a nation. We stopped dreaming. We should always have dreams.

HERB BROOKS

— — —

You take those little rascals, talk to them good, pat them on the back, let them think they are good—and they will go out and beat the biguns.

BEAR BRYANT

— — —

Life's battles don't always go to the stronger or faster man. But sooner or later the man who wins is the man who thinks he can.

VINCE LOMBARDI

The fewer rules a coach has, the fewer rules there are for players to break.

JOHN MADDEN

I let them know that I believe that they can succeed, and I'm going to be there to help them.

LENNY WILKENS

— — —

Overcoaching is the worst thing you can do to a player.

DEAN SMITH

Confidence is contagious.
So is lack of confidence.

VINCE LOMBARDI

Confidence shared is better than confidence only in yourself.

MIKE KRZYZEWSKI

A lot of other people didn't believe in [these players], but they believe in themselves. And that is all that matters.

BILL BELICHICK

— — —

Once you learn to quit, it becomes a habit.

VINCE LOMBARDI

— — —

When you have a perfect heart and perfect effort, you can't ask any more of the kids.

JIM CALHOUN

The most important thing of all for any team is a winning attitude. The coaches must have it. The players must have it. The student body must have it. If you have dedicated players who believe in themselves, you don't need a lot of talent.

BEAR BRYANT

Build up your weaknesses until they become your strong points.

KNUTE ROCKNE

Failures are expected by losers,
ignored by winners.

JOE GIBBS

— — —

You can't let praise or criticism get to you. It's a
weakness to get caught up in either one.

JOHN WOODEN

— — —

Don't worry about losing. Think about winning.

MIKE KRZYZEWSKI

LOVE

- AND -

RESPECT

ost successful coaches will tell you that if you want to motivate a player, you must first treat him with respect. Respect is integral to the success of any personal relationship; it's a fundamental component of leadership and a gateway to compliance. Take it from John Wooden, who explains, "You must have respect, which is a part of love, for those under your supervision. Then they will do what you ask and more." When we treat our children with love and respect, they'll respond in kind.

It's the principle of the Golden Rule: Do unto others as you would have them do unto you. If you want your child to respect others, respect your child. If you want him to value your perspective and experience, then it follows that you should not dismiss his. Our children are watching and listening. He will pay attention if you pay attention. Even a two-year-old appreciates on some level that if you say to him, "I don't yell at you so please don't yell at me," you are being fair and asking him to treat you as you treat him. And that line and logic applies just as well at twenty-two.

Rules are necessary in relationships, even ones rooted in a team atmosphere. You might think this would undermine the whole "team dynamic" ideal. But enforcing rules is just another way of showing that you love your child and want what's best for her. No matter the age of your child, every single limit can be explained confidently in terms of her personal safety, striving to do her best, and respecting others. For instance, Why is it time to go to bed? *Because we need rest to do our best tomorrow*. Why can't we have more candy? *It's not good for your teeth or your overall health.* Of course, your child will not always respond to your explanations with harmonious delight. She may even have a valid counter-argument that you hadn't considered.

How many times have you seen a player come to the coach and tell him about what he experienced in the game? How effective would that coach be in motivating and leading his team if he refused to listen? Create an environment in your family in which honest dialogue is encouraged and respected. But don't forget that children naturally look to parents for guidance and direction. That's why they ask so many questions in the first place. Answering them with conviction—and their best interest in mind—is as much a part of our role as parents as it is for coaches.

When you confidently explain limits to your child in honest and certain terms, you establish the fact that you are on his side. You show your child that you love and respect him, making it clear that you are less like a boss or dictator and more like a teacher or coach. When you respect your child's perspective, he will grow to understand and respect that you have his best interests in mind. You won't need to add threats. He will naturally aspire to your mutual goals.

Mutual commitment helps overcome the fear of failure—especially when people are part of a team sharing and achieving goals. It also sets the stage for open dialogue and honest conversation.

MIKE KRZYZEWSKI

— — —

What I will miss the most is building relationships with players. Those bonds are always going to be there, and they are personal. They are not based on wins and losses but on something you gave them, something you tried to do for them, something you tried to establish in those kids that would affect their lives.

ROY WILLIAMS

Deep down, your players must know you care about them. This is the most important thing. I could never get away with what I do if the players felt I didn't care for them. They know, in the long run, I'm in their corner.

BO SCHEMBECHLER

The coach should be the absolute boss, but he still should maintain an open mind.

RED AUERBACH

Build for your team a feeling of oneness, of dependence on one another and of strength to be derived by unity.

VINCE LOMBARDI

And if you see me, smile and maybe give me a hug. That's important to me too.

JIM VALVANO

— — —

Love is the force that ignites the spirit and binds teams together.

PHIL JACKSON

There are five fundamental qualities that make every team great: communication, trust, collective responsibility, caring, and pride. I like to think of each as a separate finger on the fist. Any one individually is important. But all of them together are unbeatable.

MIKE KRZYZEWSKI

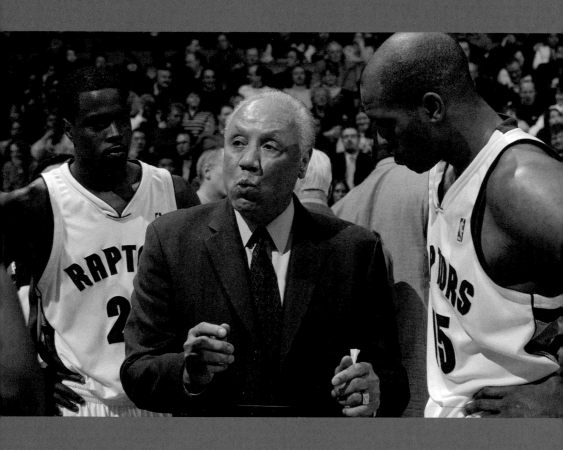

If you want it, you've got to give it.

LENNY WILKENS

Be and look prepared. Be a man of integrity. Never break your word. Don't have two sets of standards. Stand up for your players. Show them you care on and off the court.

RED AUERBACH

I motivate players through communication, being honest with them, [and] having them respect and appreciate your ability and your help.

TOMMY LASORDA

Do right. Do your best. Treat others as you want to be treated.

LOU HOLTZ

Effective teamwork begins and ends with communication.

MIKE KRZYZEWSKI

You have to communicate with people, and respect is a two-way street.

LENNY WILKENS

— — —

Coaching is a profession of love. You can't coach people unless you love them.

EDDIE ROBINSON

73

I won't accept anything less than the best a player's capable of doing, and he has the right to expect the best that I can do for him and the team.

LOU HOLTZ

Make sure that team members know they are working with you, not for you.

JOHN WOODEN

Hard work and togetherness. They go hand in hand. You need the hard work because it's such a tough atmosphere to win week in and week out. You need togetherness because you don't always win, and you gotta hang tough together.

TONY DUNGY

Humanity is the keystone that holds nations and men together. When that collapses, the whole structure crumbles. This is as true of baseball teams as any other pursuit in life.

CONNIE MACK

— — —

Motivating through fear may work in the short term to get people to do something, but over the long run I believe personal pride is a much greater motivator. It produces far better results that last for a much longer time.

JOHN WOODEN

When a leader takes responsibility for his own actions
and mistakes, he not only sets
a good example, he shows a
healthy respect for people on
his team.

MIKE KRZYZEWSKI

TEACH

– AND –

LEARN

Parenting is no easy business. It takes effort and dedication to teach our children how to thrive in this complicated world. Unfortunately, there is no single formula you can apply to every child or every situation. We learn as we go. We have to assess and adjust on the fly—take what the defense is giving us, if you will.

Lessons are taught in many different ways. There are times when you will need to trust your instincts and times when you should fight them; times when you should take action and times when you should quietly observe. Sometimes your child will need a little push and sometimes your child will need a big hug. We may not always know exactly what to do. It can be frustrating and exhausting. At times like this we need to stay positive. Take it from Michael Jordan, who said, "Never think of the consequences of failing—you will always think of a negative result. Think only positive thoughts, and your mind will gravitate towards those thoughts!" By now you know that parenting is hard work. The good news is that the more you pour your heart into it, the more your heart will be refilled with pride and joy.

Mistakes, challenges, and failures are part of growing up and part of life. Your child will fail. She will stumble. She will break down and cry. How will you respond? In order for your child to begin to see each challenge as a learning opportunity, you must first see them as teachable moments. When you treat each pitfall as a chance for your child to grow stronger and wiser, then each test is a means to strengthen your bond with your child and for her to ultimately succeed.

It's a long run. Be patient. Guide them honestly and directly. Don't take it personally if they make choices you wouldn't make. As children develop, from toddlers to teens, they learn about their world by testing limits. Think of them as junior scientists, experimenting because they have to. And when they come to you with questions, answer them honestly and carefully. When you explain the "why," you teach your child about our world and your values, and remind him that you are on his side. Be present for your child and help him learn from both success and failure. Like Red Auerbach, keep an open mind, and like Phil Jackson, keep an open heart. If you listen closely, you may just discover who the real teachers are and how much more we have to learn.

The coach is first of all a teacher.

JOHN WOODEN

You can observe a lot by just watching.

YOGI BERRA

I don't look at it like I'm on them. I'm trying to teach them. When they do something right, I try to tell them [that they're doing] something right. When they do something wrong, [I] try to coach them. This is the way I was taught and the way we've always done it.

LARRY BROWN

Coaching is about adjustments. Your game plan is only good for the first six minutes—the rest is all about adjustments.

ROY WILLIAMS

When you make a mistake, there are only three things you should ever do about it:

1. Admit it.
2. Learn from it.
3. Don't repeat it.

BEAR BRYANT

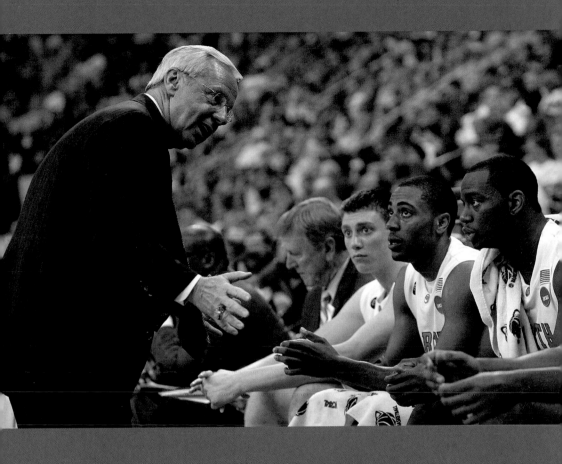

Coaches have to watch for
what they don't want to
see and listen to what they
don't want to hear.

JOHN MADDEN

I found out that if you are going to win games, you had better be ready to adapt.

SCOTTY BOWMAN

— — —

Every leader needs to remember that a healthy respect for authority takes time to develop. It's like building trust. You don't instantly have trust, it has to be earned.

MIKE KRZYZEWSKI

Discipline is not a
nasty word.

PAT RILEY

Be prepared and be honest.

JOHN WOODEN

— — —

*You can learn a line from a win and a
book from a defeat.*

PAUL BROWN

A crisis can be a momentous time for a team to grow—if a leader handles it properly.

MIKE KRZYZWESKI

When you want to win a game, you have to teach. When you lose a game, you have to learn.

LOU HOLTZ

If you're not making mistakes, then you're not doing anything. I'm positive that a doer makes mistakes.

JOHN WOODEN

What I try to do is make sense, try to be as honest as I can possibly be, and be able to communicate. I think that's the most important thing.

JOE TORRE

Failure is good. It's fertilizer. Everything I've learned about coaching, I've learned from making mistakes.

RICK PITINO

It's not what you teach, it's what you emphasize.

JOHN WOODEN

*Give people enough guidance to make
the decisions you want them to make.
Don't tell them what to do, but encourage
them to do what is best.*

JIMMY JOHNSON

Confrontation simply means meeting the
truth head-on.

MIKE KRZYZEWSKI

LIVE

- AND -

ENJOY

For children, living in the moment comes naturally. When a child looks up at the clouds or stomps in a puddle, she is not mulling over her past or worrying about her future. Sure, toddlers have less to worry about than adults, but the time and energy we spend preoccupied and fretting would undoubtedly be much better applied toward the task at hand. In sports, the ability to focus on the moment is perhaps the greatest determinant of an athlete's success. It's true in the batter's box, on the tee, at the free-throw line, and during the two-minute warning. The capacity to tune out distractions is often what separates the winners from the losers. This holds true in parenting as well. If we could all be a bit more like toddlers and savor each present moment, we would certainly find greater success at parenting.

How many times have you had the opportunity to spend time with your child only to find your mind drifting off to worries? How many times have you paid more attention to an electronic device than your child? Our gadgets and entertainment take us briefly away from stress and pressures, but ultimately they just take us away. Ask any parent who has taken their child to college about that event and their experience. I bet you'll hear the old "blink of an eye" line. We should make an effort to focus our eyes and our minds more on our children today.

When you are with your child, give him the gift of your undivided attention. Be fully present. Be conscious of the energy and tone you bring to the table. The best coaches are enthusiastic and engaged in every drill, every practice, every game. Like them, you set the tone for your family each day. Choose to enjoy each moment in their presence and bring a positive and giving spirit. When you are away from your family, be present doing your best for yourself and your family. You will find that when you are in the moment, each day will bring success.

Make a conscious effort to enjoy your child, your time together, and the journey of parenthood. Show and tell her that you are interested and that she is enjoyable. Then sit back and watch just how interesting and enjoyable she becomes. If, as Phil Jackson contends, "The ideal way to win a championship is step-by-step," then think of each moment you spend with your child as one small step. The memories and relationship you create together are your championship.

There are 86,400 seconds in a day. It's up to you to decide what to do with them.

JIM VALVANO

— — —

In basketball—as in life—true joy comes from being fully present in each and every moment, not just when things are going your way. Of course, it's no accident that things are more likely to go your way when you stop worrying about whether you're going to win or lose and focus your full attention on what's happening *right this moment.*

PHIL JACKSON

I tend to attack the challenges that are right in front of me, the ones that I have today.

MIKE TOMLIN

Winning is important to me, but what brings me real joy is the experience of being fully engaged in whatever I'm doing.

PHIL JACKSON

People who live in the past generally are afraid to compete in the present. I've got my faults, but living in the past is not one of them. There's no future in it.

SPARKY ANDERSON

— — —

The future ain't what it used to be.

YOGI BERRA

What happened yesterday is history. What happens tomorrow is a mystery. What we do today makes a difference—the precious present moment.

NICK SABAN

If you aren't fired with enthusiasm, you will be fired with enthusiasm.

VINCE LOMBARDI

The thrill isn't in the winning, it's in the doing.

CHUCK NOLL

— — —

You've got to have fun sometimes.

BILL WALSH

People who enjoy what they are doing invariably do it well.

JOE GIBBS

We'll worry about next week next week.

BILL BELICHICK

You've got to celebrate. There are some moments during the season and during a career—first big-league win, first big-league home run—that are precious. So you've got to enjoy the moment.

TONY LA RUSSA

Yesterday is a cancelled check. Today is cash on the line. Tomorrow is a promissory note.

HANK STRAM

— — —

Approach the game with no preset agendas and you'll probably come away surprised at your overall efforts.

PHIL JACKSON

— — —

At the end of the day, I'm very convinced that you're going to be judged on how you are as a husband and as a father, and not on how many bowl games [you] won.

URBAN MEYER

The key to a winning season is focusing on one opponent at a time. Winning one week at a time. Never look back and never look ahead.

CHUCK NOLL

Be where you're at.

MIKE TOMLIN

I urge all of you to enjoy your life, the precious moments you have. To spend each day with some laughter and some thought, to get your emotions going.

JIM VALVANO

— — —

After the cheers have died down and the stadium is empty, after the headlines have been written and after you are back in the quiet of your room and the championship ring has been placed on the dresser and the pomp and fanfare has faded, the enduring things that are left are: the dedication to excellence, the dedication to victory, and the dedication to doing with our lives the very best we can to make the world a better place in which to live.

VINCE LOMBARDI

Like life, basketball is messy and unpredictable. It has its way with you, no matter how hard you try to control it. The trick is to experience each moment with a clear mind and open heart. When you do that, the game—and life—will take care of itself.

PHIL JACKSON

Make each day your masterpiece.

JOHN WOODEN

Photo Credits